Abraham Lincoln
A Great American Life

L. L. Owens

Perfection Learning®

Cover Design: Alan Stanley and Deborah Lea Bell
Inside Design: Deborah Lea Bell
Inside Illustration: Michael A. Aspengren

Image credits: Tria Giovan/Corbis front cover (background image)

ArtToday: pp. 1, 2, 5, 6, 7, 8, 9, 10, 11, 12, 13, 14, 15, 16, 17, 18, 20, 21, 23, 24, 25, 26, 27, 28, 30, 31, 32, 33, 35, 37, 38 (top), 39, 40, 41, 42 (statue), 43, 44, 45, 47, 49, 50, 51, 52, 54, 56 **Digital Stock:** p. 48 **IMSI MasterPhotos:** back cover (background image) **LOC:** pp. 36, 42 (Gettysburg Address)

About the Author

Lisa L. Owens grew up in the Midwest. She studied English and journalism at the University of Iowa. She currently works as an editor in Seattle.

Other books by Ms.Owens include *Code of the Drum* and *Brothers at War*.

For information, contact
Perfection Learning® Corporation,
1000 North Second Avenue, P.O. Box 500,
Logan, Iowa 51546-0500.
Phone: 1-800-831-4190 • Fax: 1-712-644-2392

PB ISBN-10: 0-7891-5162-6 ISBN-13: 978-0-7891-5162-9
RLB ISBN-10: 0-7807-9307-2 ISBN-13: 978-0-7807-9307-1

7 8 9 10 11 12 PP 18 17 16 15 14 13

Table of Contents

CHAPTER 1

Baby Abraham

February 12, 1809

It was a Sunday. And it was the day Abraham Lincoln was born.

Abe's parents were Thomas and Nancy. They lived in Hardin County, Kentucky. Their home was a log cabin. Thomas was a farmer and a carpenter.

Dennis Hanks was Nancy's cousin. He saw Abe that first day. He said, "He'll never come to much."

Years later, Dennis explained why he'd said that. He said that Abe was "the puniest, cryin'est little youngster I ever saw."

Dennis was wrong. Abe grew up to be one of the greatest men in American history!

CHAPTER 2

The Early Years

The Lincolns moved to Indiana when Abe was seven. Sarah, Abe's sister, was ten.

Their new home was in the woods. They planned to farm. So the land needed to be cleared.

Abe was big for his age. He was very strong too. He could easily handle an ax.

Soon he was put to work. His father cut trees. And Abe chopped out the undergrowth.

Abe's Earliest Memory of Indiana

One day, Abe spotted a flock of wild turkeys. They were just outside the cabin.

He asked his mom, "May I use Father's gun?"

"Yes," she said.

Abe stayed inside the cabin. He aimed at the flock through a crack in the wall. Then he fired the gun.

Abe hit and killed one of the turkeys!

He went outside to collect it. Up close, he thought the bird was beautiful. He was upset. He wished he hadn't killed it.

Abe said later, "I never again pulled a trigger on any larger game."

Sadly, Abe's mother died in 1818. The whole family was brokenhearted.

About a year later, Abe's father took a trip to Kentucky. He wanted a new wife. He also wanted a mother for his children.

He soon married Sarah Bush Johnston. He and Nancy had known Sarah and her husband. And now Sarah was a **widow**.

Abe and his sister welcomed Sarah and her three children. They were glad to have a new mom. And they were happy to have new sisters and a brother. Their names were Elizabeth, Matilda, and John.

Nancy died from *milk sickness*. It's a disease. She got it from drinking milk.

But not just any milk. The milk she drank came from a cow. It had eaten white snakeroot.

White snakeroot was poisonous. And it had infected the milk.

The Lincolns were poor. So Abe worked to help support the family. He worked even when he was young.

That meant he couldn't go to school very often.

Still, Abe loved to learn. He spent every free moment reading. Sometimes he'd walk for many miles just to borrow a new book!

Abe's days were spent working hard. He worked from morning till evening.

He'd eat supper with the family. Then he'd sit in front of the fire. And he'd read late into the night.

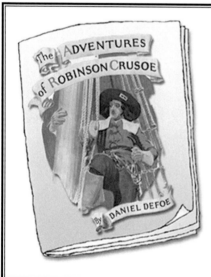

These books shaped Abe's education. He referred to them all his life.

Aesop's Fables

The Bible

Life of Washington

The Pilgrim's Progress

The Adventures of
  Robinson Crusoe

John couldn't believe his brother's energy. For John was always tired after a day's work. He usually went straight to bed after supper.

Abe was tired too. But he was different. To him, learning was an exciting thing. So he made the time to do it.

Abe learned about history, literature, and grammar. He did this all on his own. He had a great memory.

Neighbors loved to hear him talk about his studies. They were amazed at the things he knew.

Lincoln once said . . .

"Leave nothing for tomorrow which can be done today."

—July 1850

Abe once said this about his memory.

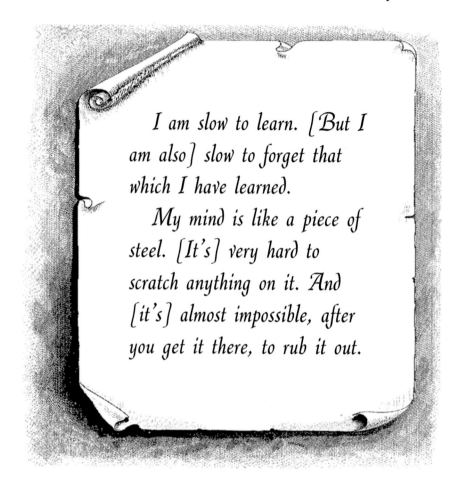

> *I am slow to learn. [But I am also] slow to forget that which I have learned.*
>
> *My mind is like a piece of steel. [It's] very hard to scratch anything on it. And [it's] almost impossible, after you get it there, to rub it out.*

Abe's dad never really understood Abe's thirst for knowledge.

His stepmother Sarah did, though. She urged him to follow his interests. Abe was forever grateful.

CHAPTER 3

Growing Up

Times were still hard for the Lincolns. Abe did all he could to help.

At 15, he started working for neighbors. It was a way for him to earn extra money.

He did things like plowing and planting. He did odd jobs too. He did whatever people needed.

The neighbors were happy with Abe's work. They trusted him. And they knew he always did his best.

In 1828, Abe's sister Sarah died while giving birth. That was a sad day for the Lincolns and Sarah's husband.

Abe was 19 then. He missed his sister for the rest of his life.

Abe continued his studies. He wanted to make the world a better place. So he tried to learn as much as possible.

That spring, Abe delivered **produce** to New Orleans. It was a long trip. He went with his friend Allen Gentry. They traveled by flatboat.

On the way, they were attacked. Seven men tried to rob them. But Abe and Allen fought back. They saved their **cargo**. And they were able to sell it in New Orleans.

Abe saw a slave **auction** in New Orleans.

It was awful. White people were buying black people.

Lincoln once said . . .

"Whenever I hear anyone arguing for slavery, I feel a strong impulse to see it tried on him personally."
—*March 17, 1865*

The black people were in chains. They couldn't break away. The people who bought the black people used them as slaves.

It was hard for Abe to watch. He knew slavery was wrong. His family had never believed in it.

But slavery was legal in the South. So Abe couldn't do anything to stop it. At least there was nothing he could do right then.

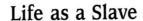

Life as a Slave

Most slaves were taken to **plantations**. They did all the hard labor. But their white owners kept the **profits**.

Slaves lived in constant fear. They were treated like animals.

They suffered from hunger. They had cramped, dirty living spaces. Sometimes their babies were taken from them and sold.

Slaves had no freedom or rights. They had to do whatever white people said. If they didn't, they were punished.

They were whipped. They were beaten. And many were killed.

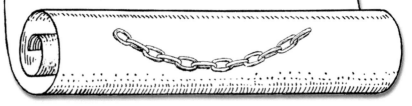

CHAPTER 4

Two Presidents Agree

Honesty Is the Best Policy

Guess what? You and Abe have something in common.

Think about it. You're reading about a president from long ago. Abe did that too. He read about President Washington.

Young George was known for his honesty.

Here is a story that Abe probably read. In it, George tells the truth. Even though it hurts a little.

George Washington and the Cherry Tree

As a boy, George received an ax. It was a gift from his father.

George loved the ax. He was eager to use it.

He was alone in the yard one afternoon. And no one was looking. So he went over to a cherry tree.

George swung the ax. He hit the trunk again and again.

Soon he saw the damage he had caused. He stopped. And he walked away.

"I hope no one notices," he thought.

His father noticed, of course.

"George!" he called out.

"Yes, Father?"

"Come here, Son."

George did as he was told.

His father said, "Look at this cherry tree. There are fresh cuts all over the trunk. Do you know what happened?"

George was quiet for a moment. He knew he had to confess. So he took a deep breath.

Then he said, "I cannot tell a lie! I cut it with my new ax. I am sorry!"

His father thanked him for telling the truth. "I know it was hard, Son. But you did the right thing. And now you will accept your punishment."

"Yes, sir," George agreed.

Some say that this is just a **myth**. That it didn't really happen. Who knows?

In any case, George Washington stands for honesty. And cherry pie is considered a patriotic treat!

You've probably heard Abe called "Honest Abe." He earned that nickname. Like George Washington, he believed in telling the truth—always!

Now here's a story from Abe's youth. It's about honesty. And it involves an ax. It's kind of like George's tale!

Abe's Brotherly Advice

Abe's sister Matilda liked to sneak away from her chores. One fall morning, she decided to follow Abe. Her mom had told her not to.

Abe left at dawn. His ax was on his shoulder. He walked deep into the woods. He was going to clear a spot of land.

Abe had no idea that 'Tilda was behind him. He whistled and walked for a while.

Without warning, 'Tilda ran forward. She jumped onto Abe's back. The two fell to the ground.

During the fall, Abe's ax slipped. It cut 'Tilda's ankle. She cried out in pain. Blood gushed from the wound.

Abe quickly ripped up his shirt. He stopped the bleeding and tied up his sister's ankle.

Abe was relieved. The injury was not serious.

Finally, 'Tilda calmed down. Abe asked, "What are you going to tell your mother?"

'Tilda was worried. She asked, "Can't I just tell her I hurt myself with the ax?"

Abe looked at her sternly. He shook his head no.

"That would be the truth," she said.

Gently, Abe answered, "Yes. That's the truth. But it's not all the truth."

He continued. "Tell the whole truth, 'Tilda. And trust your good mother for the rest."

Matilda had no choice. She told her mother exactly what had happened.

And yes, she was punished. But this time, she really learned a lesson!

CHAPTER 5

An Amazing Career

In 1830, the Lincolns moved 200 miles to Illinois. They settled near Decatur. Abe was 21 years old.

The next year, Abe moved to New Salem, Illinois. He was finally on his own. He held several jobs in town.

He worked as a **rail-splitter**, store clerk, and store owner. He was a county **surveyor** and a **postmaster**. Abe also served in the Black Hawk War.

He became a great lawyer. He made many friends. And his political career took off.

Abe moved to Springfield in 1837. He married Mary Todd in 1842.

Mary was proud of Abe. She supported his career.

The couple had four sons. They led a happy life together.

Abe was successful. He made a good living. So he was able to give his family things he'd never had.

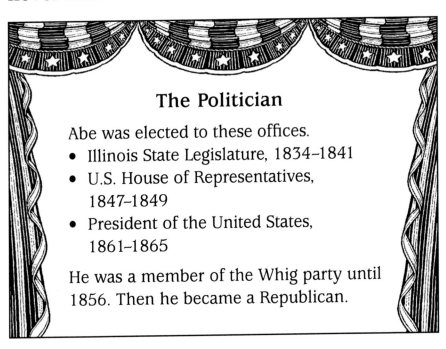

The Politician

Abe was elected to these offices.
- Illinois State Legislature, 1834–1841
- U.S. House of Representatives, 1847–1849
- President of the United States, 1861–1865

He was a member of the Whig party until 1856. Then he became a Republican.

Abe and Mary's Children

Robert—
born 1843; died 1926

Edward "Eddie"—
born 1846; died 1850

William "Willie"—
born 1850; died 1862

Thomas "Tad"—
born 1853; died 1871

They lived in a fine home. The boys went to school. And Abe and Mary spent lots of time with their children.

Abe won the election for president on November 6, 1860. He beat Stephen Douglas, John Bell, and John C. Breckenridge.

Abe was now the 16th president of the United States. His vice president was Hannibal Hamlin.

In February 1861, the Lincolns left Springfield. They were headed for Washington, D.C.

Abe was sworn in on March 4. He would deal with many problems as the nation's leader.

CHAPTER 6

Lincoln's Whiskers

Abe was in his fifties when he grew his first beard. Why did he grow one then? A girl named Grace Bedell asked him to!

Grace wrote to Abe in 1860. It was a few weeks before the presidential election.

She asked him to grow a beard. She thought he would get more votes if he did.

On the next page is an edited version of Grace's letter.

October 15, 1860

Dear Sir,

My father has just gotten home from the fair. He brought home your picture.

I am a little girl. I am 11 years old. I want you to be president of the United States very much.

I hope you won't think me very bold to write to you. You are such a great man.

Have you a little girl about my age? If so, give her my love. And tell her to write to me if you cannot answer this letter.

I have four brothers. Part of them will vote for you. If you let your whiskers grow, I will try to get the rest of them to vote for you.

You would look a great deal better with a beard. Your face is so thin.

All the ladies like whiskers. They would tease their husbands to vote for you. Then you would be president.

My father is going to vote for you. If I were a man, I would vote for you too. I will try to get everyone to vote for you that I can I think of.

When you write, direct your letter to Grace Bedell, Westfield, New York.

I must not write any more. Answer this letter right off.

Good-bye,
Grace Bedell

In the early 1990s, Grace's original letter was sold. The price was $1 million!

The letter is now part of the Burton Historical Collection. It is kept at the Detroit Public Library.

Abe answered Grace's letter on October 19.
His letter read

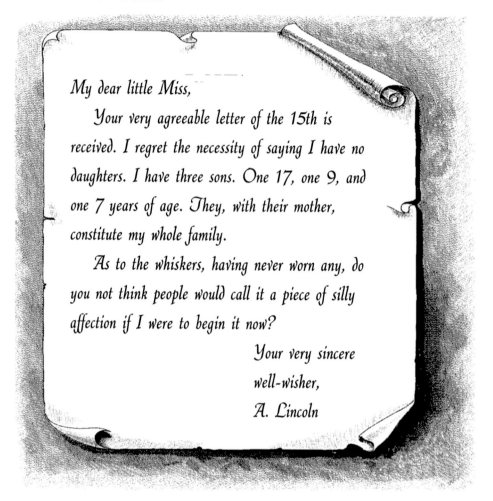

My dear little Miss,

Your very agreeable letter of the 15th is received. I regret the necessity of saying I have no daughters. I have three sons. One 17, one 9, and one 7 years of age. They, with their mother, constitute my whole family.

As to the whiskers, having never worn any, do you not think people would call it a piece of silly affection if I were to begin it now?

Your very sincere
well-wisher,
A. Lincoln

On February 16, 1861, Abe was on his way to the White House. He'd won the election. He was the new president.

His train stopped in Westfield, New York. He stepped onto the platform and waved to the crowd.

The Trendsetter

Abe was a very popular figure. He was admired by many. People were interested in everything he did.

His new beard caused quite a stir. Before long, lots of men had grown them.

Wearing a beard was a national trend. It was all because of one girl's request!

Just for Fun

Most pictures of Abe show him with a beard. How many can you find of him without one?

Grace was there. She gasped when she saw him. He had a full beard!

"Grace Bedell!" Abe called out. She rushed forward.

Abe greeted her with a kiss on the cheek. "I took your advice, Grace," he said.

Grace never forgot that exciting day!

CHAPTER 7

The Many Sides of a Great Man

Abraham Lincoln had many good traits. He was easy to talk to. He was easy to listen to. And he was very easy to like.

He had many hobbies. He did lots of different things well. That's part of what made him so interesting.

Here are just a few of Abe's talents.

Abe the Storyteller

People loved Abe's stories. He told them to anyone who'd listen. Everywhere he went, he told stories!

His stories were meant to entertain. And they did. But they often made an important point too. Such as

- why he should win a legal case
- why he held certain opinions
- what his political views were
- how he made decisions during the Civil War

Abe the Writer

Abe wrote often. He wrote letters. He wrote two **autobiographies**. He also wrote essays. He even wrote poetry.

On the next page is one of his poems. He wrote it when he was 37. He had just visited his boyhood home in Indiana.

The poem is about memories and feelings stirred up during his trip. Some were happy. And some were sad.

My childhood's home I see again,
And sadden with the view;
And still, as memory crowds my brain,
There's pleasure in it too.

O Memory! thou midway world
'Twixt earth and paradise,
Where things decayed and loved ones lost
In dreamy shadows rise.

The friends I left that parting day
How changed, as time has sped!
Young childhood grown, strong manhood gray,
And half of all are dead.

I hear the loved survivors tell
How nought from death could save,
Till every sound appears a knell,
And every spot a grave.

I range the fields with pensive tread,
And pace the hollow rooms,
And feel (companions of the dead)
I'm living in the tombs.

Abe the Inventor

Abe was good at solving problems. One day, he thought of a way to help boats float higher in the water. He invented the **buoy** system.

The system could be attached to a boat. When the boat passed through shallow water, it floated higher.

That way, it wouldn't scrape against a sandbar. And it wouldn't hit the rocky river bottom.

Abe's idea worked. He was granted a **patent**. Then he got credit for inventing the device.

He was the only president ever granted a patent. It was U.S. Patent Number 6,469. He received it on May 22, 1849.

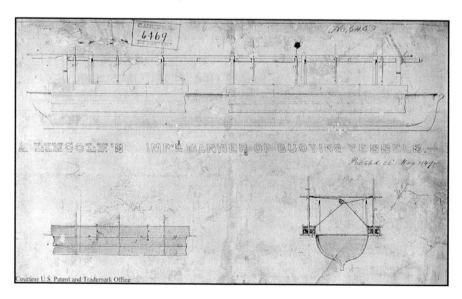

CHAPTER 8

The Civil War Years

In 1860, several Southern states left the Union. They were unhappy. They didn't want Abe to be the new president. They didn't like his policies.

For one thing, Abe wanted to end slavery. But Southern slave owners didn't.

They thought owning black people was their "right." So they decided to form their own country.

Abe wanted the North and the South to stay together. He knew it would be dangerous to split one strong nation in two.

He also believed in the United States government. And he believed in the will of the people.

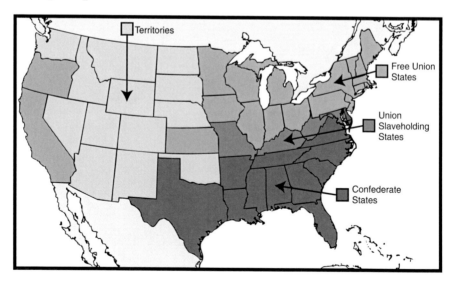

Abe thought the South should just wait for their chance to vote him out of office.

In 1861, Southern states attacked Fort Sumter. Abe had no choice. He prepared the army. And the war between the North and South began.

Lincoln once said . . .

"A house divided against itself cannot stand."

—*June 16, 1858*

Time to Vote

The Union held its 1864 presidential election. Even though the Civil War was raging.

Abe was reelected. He ran on the National Union ticket. His running mate was Andrew Johnson.

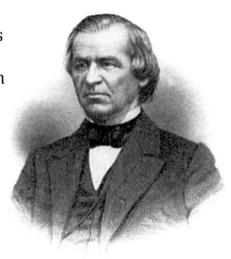

The Civil War lasted four long years. About 600,000 soldiers died. It was a bitter struggle for both sides.

Finally, it ended April 9, 1865. General Lee **surrendered** to General Grant. The North had won.

Slavery ended. And the North and South were rejoined.

The Other President

Anti-Union forces were called the Confederacy. They formed their own nation. It was called the Confederate States of America. Richmond, Virginia, was named the capital.

Jefferson Davis was elected president. He held this post until the war ended.

Four score and seven years ago our fathers brought forth, upon this continent, a new nation, conceived in Liberty, and dedicated to the proposition that all men are created equal.

Now we are engaged in a great civil war, testing whether that nation, or any nation, so conceived, and so dedicated, can long endure. We are met here on a great battlefield of that war. We have come to dedicate a portion of it as a final resting place for those who here gave their lives that that nation might live. It is altogether fitting and proper that we should do this.

But in a larger sense we can not dedicate— we can not consecrate— we can not hallow this ground. The brave men, living and dead, who struggled here, have consecrated it far above our poor power to add or detract. The world will little note, nor long remember, what we say here, but can never forget what they did here. It is for us, the living, rather to be dedicated here to the unfinished work, which they have, thus far, so nobly carried on. It is rather for us to be here dedicated to the great task remaining before us— that from these honored dead we take increased devotion to that cause for which they here gave the last full measure of devotion— that we here highly resolve that these dead shall not have died in vain; that this nation shall have a new birth of freedom; and that this government of the people, by the people, for the people, shall not perish from the earth.

CHAPTER 9

The Gettysburg Address

Abe gave many speeches. But the Gettysburg Address is his most famous one. This is how it begins.

Four score and seven years ago, our fathers brought forth on this continent a new nation, conceived in Liberty, and dedicated to the proposition that all men are created equal.

Have you heard it?

Abe gave the address on November 19, 1863. He was **dedicating** a cemetery. It was for soldiers who had died at the Battle of Gettysburg.

Abe wasn't the only speaker that day. The main speaker was Edward Everett. He was the most popular speaker of the era.

Edward spoke for two hours. There were 15,000 people at the ceremony. They got bored and restless.

Some people left. Others searched the battlefield. They looked for bullets and other **souvenirs**.

Finally, Edward finished. People sang a hymn. Then Abe started to speak.

People wanted to hear him. So they started rushing back to the platform.

It was a great speech. But it lasted just three minutes! Many people missed it. They just couldn't get back in time.

Gettysburg: A Deadly Battle

One out of every three Confederate soldiers died.

One out of every five Union soldiers died.

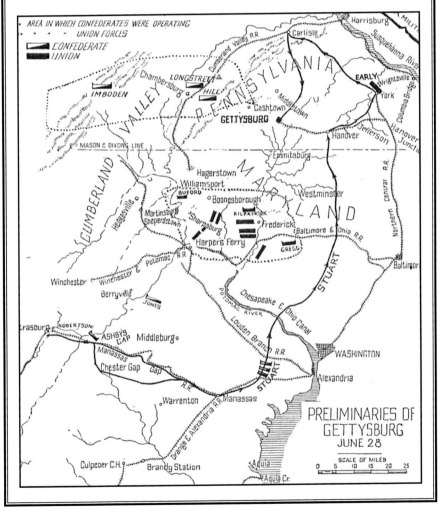

The Gettysburg Address is often quoted. And people still study it.

What made it so great?

For one thing, the speech was rewritten several times. Right up until the morning of the 19th. Abe wanted it to be just right.

Also, Abe practiced it. So he knew it very well.

The 270-word speech was very clear. It summed up the crowd's beliefs. Abe used simple language. So everyone understood his message.

CHAPTER 10

The Assassination of a President

April 14, 1865

Abe felt glad. The war was over. It was time for the nation to heal.

That night, Abe and Mary saw a play. It was called *Our American Cousin.* They watched from the State Box at Ford's Theatre.

During the third act, John Wilkes Booth entered the State Box. He was behind the Lincolns. They didn't hear him. He held a knife and a gun.

Booth shot the president in the head. The exact time was 10:13 p.m.

Mary screamed. People rushed to Abe's side.

Abe was in a coma. He was taken to a house across the street. Doctors tended to him. Friends and family gathered.

Abe never woke up again.

Booth escaped. He jumped from the balcony. One of his spurs caught in a flag. Booth fell to the floor with a broken leg. But he was able to make it to the back door where he mounted a horse and fled.

Booth later died in a fire during a shootout with federal troops .

A Booth Saves a Lincoln

Edwin Booth once saved Robert Lincoln's life. Robert was Abe's son. And Edwin was John Wilkes Booth's brother.

One night, Robert planned to travel from New York to Washington. It was 1863 or 1864. He was at a railroad station in Jersey City.

Robert waited to buy a ticket. He wanted a sleeping car. The station was crowded.

Robert stood at the end of the platform. There was a space between the platform and a train car.

Suddenly, the train moved. Robert lost his balance. He fell. Right into the open space. He thought he would get run over!

Edwin saw Robert fall. He quickly reached out. He grabbed Robert by the collar. He pulled him up and saved his life.

Robert was grateful. Edwin was glad he'd been there to help.

Neither knew that a Lincoln would soon die at the hands of a Booth.

Edwin Booth

President Abraham Lincoln died at 7:22 a.m. on April 15.

Edwin Stanton was Lincoln's War Secretary. He stayed with Lincoln right up to his death. Then he said sadly, "Now he belongs to the ages."

A Brief Escape

John Wilkes Booth got away! He fled Washington on horseback. He rode off with David Herold. Herold, with others, had planned the murder.

Union troops searched for Abe's killers. On April 26, they caught Booth and Herold. The men were hiding in a Virginia tobacco shed.

Herold turned himself in. But Booth didn't. The troops shot into the shed to bring him out. Then they set fire to it.

John Wilkes Booth died that day. Some say he died from a gunshot wound. Others say he burned to death.

Lincoln's family–and his country–were shocked and saddened. A long period of mourning followed.

Mary's grief overpowered her. She couldn't even attend Abe's funeral or his burial.

This was the first presidential **assassination** in U.S. history. And it would never be forgotten. People were angry. Abe missed out on the good things to come.

Abe didn't get to see so many things. He didn't see the rebuilding of his nation and the legal end to slavery. He didn't even see his son Robert's success as a lawyer.

On December 6, 1865, the 13th **Amendment** was **ratified**. That means that the law ending slavery went into effect.

Abraham Lincoln would have been proud.

Glossary

amendment	an addition to the U.S. Constitution
assassinate	to kill
auction	an event at which items are sold to the highest bidder
autobiography	a person's self-written life story
buoy	something that floats
cargo	a load
dedicate	to name in honor of a person, group, or idea
myth	a traditional story about a historical event or person that explains a belief, practice, or natural happening
patent	a government document that gives only an inventor the right to make, use, or sell his or her invention
plantation	a large Southern farm

postmaster	a person who is in charge of a postal zone
produce	farm goods
profits	money left from selling goods after expenses have been subtracted
rail-splitter	a person who makes fence rails from logs
ratify	to formally approve
souvenir	an item that reminds a person of a place or an event
surrender	to admit defeat
surveyor	one who measures and keeps track of land plots
widow	a woman whose husband has died